Contents

Turn It Down!

Listen. Do you hear something? Chances are, the answer is yes. Sound is all around us. In fact, in many places, complete silence can be hard to find.

Many of the sounds we hear around us are unwanted sounds, or **noise**. In towns, noise comes mostly from traffic, building works and people. Noise in the countryside can come from farm equipment, passing trains and low-flying planes.

Both the countryside and cities experience noise pollution.

Unfortunately many people do not realize that noise can be dangerous. Of course, noise can be irritating. Many people think too much noise, called **noise pollution**, harms the environment. Loud or prolonged noise can damage your hearing and even threaten your health. In this book, you will learn more about the dangers of noise and how to avoid them. Perhaps you will see that protecting yourself from too much noise is a sound decision!

The volume control of personal stereos are often turned up to dangerous levels.

Sound Versus Noise

No one would argue against the importance of sound. Sound helps you to understand the world around you. Some sounds, such as speech, allow you to communicate with others. Other sounds, such as car horns and alarms, are useful as warnings. Still other sounds, such as music, entertain you and help you to relax.

Yet speech, alarms and music are sometimes considered **noise**, too. Sound becomes noise when it is unwanted. (In fact, the word *noise* comes from the Latin word *nausea*, which means "seasickness".) For example, everyday speech is a useful, helpful sound that people depend on to communicate. However, in a theatre or a library, everyday speech becomes noise.

Are these sounds or noises?
It depends on your point of view.

Just as not all sound can be considered noise, not all noise can be considered harmful. Although most people would agree that the screech of fingernails on a board is an unwanted sound, the noise itself is not going to hurt you. However, the sound of a drill breaking up concrete can be harmful. Usually, noise is harmful only if it is loud. The louder a noise, the more likely it is to damage your hearing or health.

Some irritating noises, such as the squeaking of chalk on a board, are harmless. Others, such as the pounding of a pneumatic drill, can be harmful.

How Loud Is Too Loud?

At what point does a **noise** become too loud? To answer that question, it's important to know a little about how sound works.

Sound waves spread from the source of a noise like ripples in water.

Sound Waves

Sound is produced when an object **vibrates**, or moves backwards and forwards very quickly. This movement also makes the air around the object vibrate. The air transmits the vibrations in the form of **sound waves**. Most of the sounds that people hear travel in the same way that ripples spread out from a pebble thrown into a pond.

How Sound Waves Are Made

Think of how a guitar string vibrates when plucked. The vibration causes air particles around the string to move. These particles hit nearby particles, and those particles hit particles near them. The particles become **compressed**, or squeezed together.

As the vibrating string moves back, it leaves space into which the particles can spread, separating them again from nearby particles, which in turn separate from particles next to them, and so on. The combination of compressing and separating of particles creates a sound wave that travels away from the vibrating string.

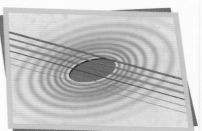

Air particles vibrate to produce sound when a guitar string is plucked.

Sound waves can be compared to ocean waves. The highest point of the wave is called the **crest**. The lowest point is called the **trough**. If the sound wave has a low crest and trough then the sound is soft. If the sound wave has a hight crest and trough then the sound is loud.

The difference in height between the crest and the trough depends on how compressed the particles of air are. The more they are compressed, the more energy the sound wave has and the louder the sound it produces.

Sound Waves and Loudness

Different sounds have differently shaped waves.

This sound has a low crest and trough and produces a soft sound.

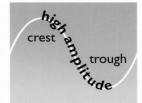

This sound has a high crest and trough and produces a loud sound.

When you **amplify** a sound, you make it louder. On some kinds of electronic equipment, the user controls the amount of sound amplification.

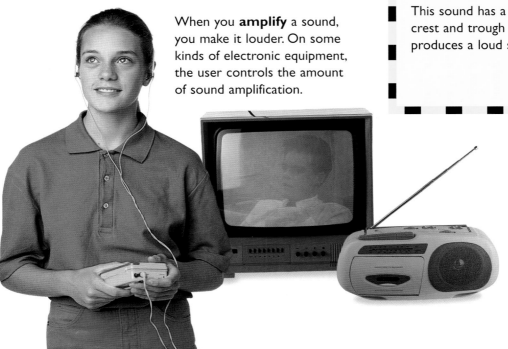

Measuring Loudness

Units called **decibels** (dB) are used to measure the loudness of a sound. A soft whisper measures 30 dB; a conversation measures about 60 dB. A prolonged sound of 80 dB is loud enough to cause pain or even damage to the ear.

Surprisingly, quite a few familiar sounds are louder than 80 dB. For example, the movements of a large truck or the **noise** from building sites all exceed this level. Sound coming through the headphones of a personal stereo set at medium volume can reach levels of more than 90 dB. So save your ears and turn it down.

The Decibel Scale	
dB	**EXAMPLE**
0	Softest sound a human can hear
30	Low whispering
40	Quiet bank, living room
50	Refrigerator, far-off traffic
60	Talking, nearby air conditioner
70	Noisy cafeteria, heavy traffic
80	Nearby alarm clock, city traffic
90	Blender, lawnmower, truck traffic
100	Music heard on headphones, chainsaw
120	Loud thunderclap, music heard near speakers at a rock concert
140	Aeroplane, gunshot
180	Rocket launch

Rocket launches are among the loudest sounds humans have ever produced.

Reflection and Absorption

Sound waves can be reflected or absorbed as they travel. An echo is an example of sound **reflection**. It is caused by sound waves bouncing off a hard surface. Sound reflection makes it possible for you to hear your own voice come back when you yell, "Hello!" in a big empty room.

Think about how noisy a cafeteria can be. The hard plastic furniture, plastic trays, linoleum floor and smooth walls are all surfaces that reflect sound. Soft materials such as curtains, screens, carpets and upholstered furniture **absorb** sound. These absorbent materials soak up some of the energy of sound waves and decrease noise.

A squash court's smooth walls and floor don't absorb sound well, making the court noisy.

Your Hearing at Risk

Certain kinds of **noise** can have serious effects on your hearing. One common cause of ear damage is exposure to loud noises over a long period of time.

Hearing Basics

To understand why noise can do so much damage to your hearing, it's important to know how the human ear works. The ear has three parts: the outer, middle and inner ear. The outer or external part of the ear is called the pinna (or auricle). This flap of skin and cartilage that surrounds the opening of the ear canal works like a funnel to catch and reflect **sound waves** down into the ear canal.

pinna

The ear canal is a narrow tube that is closed off at one end by the eardrum. Sound waves enter the ear and travel down the canal to the eardrum. The waves make the eardrum vibrate. Tiny bones called ossicles transmit the vibrations to the inner ear.

The cochlea (KOK-lee-uh) is a spiral-shaped structure in the inner ear that contains fluid and thousands of extremely sensitive hair cells. Vibrations move through the fluid inside the cochlea, creating ripples. The ripples cause the fluid to move bundles of hair cells that line the inside of the cochlea. The hair bundles turn the vibrations into nerve impulses that are sent to the brain, where they are interpreted as sound.

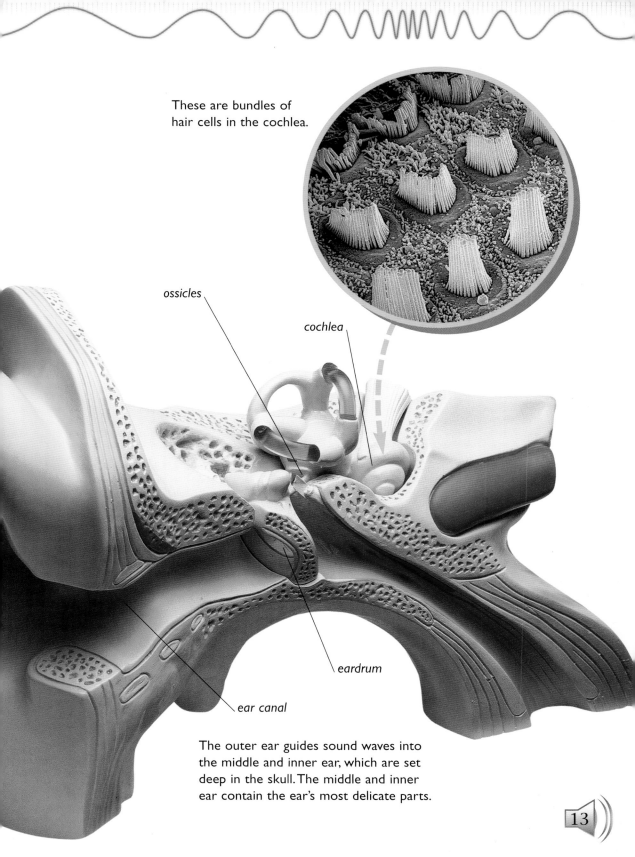

These are bundles of
hair cells in the cochlea.

ossicles

cochlea

eardrum

ear canal

The outer ear guides sound waves into
the middle and inner ear, which are set
deep in the skull. The middle and inner
ear contain the ear's most delicate parts.

Damaging Noise

Injury, illness and age can all cause hearing loss. However, the biggest threat to your hearing is exposure to loud sounds for long periods of time. In the United States alone, it's estimated that between 10 million and 17 million people suffer from some form of hearing loss caused by excessive **noise**.

Why is **noise pollution** so dangerous? High-**decibel** sounds can place too much strain on the sensitive and delicate parts of the inner ear. When a noise is too loud, it begins to kill hair cells in the inner ear. The longer you are exposed to the loud noise, the more hair cells are destroyed. As the number of living hair cells decreases, so does your ability to hear.

Over time, exposure to sound levels of 80 dB for 8 hours a day can cause **tinnitus**, a ringing, buzzing or roaring sensation in the ears or head. Repeated exposure to sound levels higher than 80 dB can do even more damage.

Everyday items such as alarm clocks and stereos can create high levels of noise. Similarly, city traffic has decibel levels that – at best – irritate your ears.

More frightening are the dangerous decibel levels at some cinemas, concerts and sporting events. Exposure to these extremely loud noises can cause long-term damage to your hearing. What's more, a sudden loud noise of 120 dB or higher can instantly cause permanent tinnitus or hearing loss.

Symptoms of Hearing Loss or Damage

- You experience ringing, tingling or pain in one or both ears.
- Sounds seem to be muffled.
- Quiet sounds are hard or impossible to hear.
- One or both ears feels plugged.
- Your ability to hear seems to come and go.

Hearing aids can help people who have some hearing loss.

Amplified music at concerts can be extremely damaging to your hearing.

Protecting Your Ears

No one would advise a cyclist to ride a bike without putting on a helmet. A football player wouldn't enter a match without pulling on shin guards. A skier would never zoom down a mountain without wearing goggles.

Yet, have you ever considered inserting earplugs before watching an explosive action thriller? Many high-tech movie sound systems can reach levels of 85 dB and beyond. Two hours of exposure to that much **noise** is definitely not healthy for your hearing. However, the chances are that you do not even own a pair of earplugs.

Airport workers are not allowed near aeroplanes without ear protection.

Hearing loss may be the number one disability in the world. However, hearing loss and **tinnitus** caused by exposure to high-**decibel** sounds can be prevented. Here's what you can do and when to do it.

First, you should own earplugs. Earplugs are the easiest and most useful tool you can use to protect yourself against harmful noise. Usually made of foam or a gel-like form of silicone, earplugs are small inserts that fit snugly into the outer ear canal. They muffle, or reduce, noise before it reaches your inner ear.

Earplugs often come in different sizes, so it's important to choose a size that fits comfortably in your ear. Different kinds of earplugs also reduce different amounts of noise. In many areas of the world, earplugs have a Noise Reduction Rating (NRR) that gives you an idea of the number of decibels the earplugs filter from your ears. Earplugs with an NRR of 25, for example, reduce the amount of noise entering your inner ear by about 25 dB. Many earplugs can reduce the amount of noise you hear by more than 30 dB.

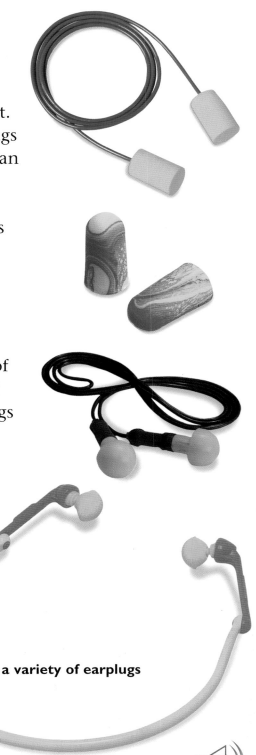

a variety of earplugs

Another way to protect your hearing is to be aware of the harmful **noises** in your environment. For example, if you are going to a concert, think about how loud the musician or band is likely to be. (Many rock bands play at **decibel** levels of more than 100 dB.) Prepare by wearing your earplugs.

Also, consider the noise in your home. You'd be surprised at how loud a television, radio, vacuum cleaner or other everyday household appliance can be. If you can't easily carry on a conversation with someone who's at least a metre away, it's likely that the sound levels in the room are at or above 85 dB.

Try to keep your television, stereo and computer volumes at a low level. Avoid having too many noise-producing machines running at the same time.

Common household appliances, such as blenders, can create noises that are so loud you have to shout to be heard over them.

Hazardous to Your Health

Loss of hearing is a big concern when it comes to noise. However, it certainly is not the only concern. A jet engine that drowns you out when you're talking on the telephone can annoy you. A tap that drips all night can keep you awake. These examples of noise may not threaten your hearing, but they can still do damage in other ways such as anxiety, depression and headaches.

Can Noise Hurt Your Pet?

Noise can harm animals, too. In the wild, a loud noise can mask the sounds that animals use to hunt for prey, escape from predators and communicate with one another. Fireworks can frighten or panic both wild animals and pets. Even underwater noise caused by ship engines and sonar can be harmful to whales, porpoises and other marine mammals.

Over time, exposure to loud noise can have the same result in many animals as it does in humans: hearing loss.

Finding a quiet place to do homework is important.

Noise can make you irritable and less productive. Have you ever been studying in a noisy place and found that it was almost impossible to concentrate? Do you sometimes feel more frustrated or get angry with people around you in a noisy place? Some of your reactions may have come from your noisy surroundings.

It is important to have quiet time each day to rest or study. Remember that sounds are directed through your ears and into your brain through nerve endings. Too much noise can confuse your brain as it tries to focus on too many things at once. Therefore spend time in a quiet environment to give your brain a rest.

Noise in the Workplace

Some people have jobs that expose them to unhealthy levels of sound. Airport workers, carpenters, builders, factory workers, miners, truck drivers, rubbish collectors and others can develop problems caused by noise. Safety standards require many employers to provide ear protection to use in the workplace. However, it is the responsibility of each worker to use the safety equipment.

This worker protects his ears while using a chainsaw.

Studies have shown that noise may be linked to many different health problems. People exposed to constant sources of noise report more headaches, insomnia, accidents and anxiety. Exposure to long periods of noise can cause problems related to heart rate, high blood pressure and digestion. It can cause exhaustion as well.

Noise can make us tense and angry. Knowing that noise can affect your health may encourage you to find ways to guard against its damaging effects.

A dripping tap is well known for being an irritating noise and can cause stress levels to increase.

Noise Pollution: A Growing Concern

Noise in the environment comes from many different sources. Sometimes we add noise to the environment ourselves, such as when we operate noisy equipment.

At other times, we experience noise that comes from someone or something out of our control. Second-hand noise can also affect our bodies and our environment. **Noise pollution** cannot be seen. It does not leave a visible trace, such as a smoky haze over a city. Noise pollution is also hard to measure. It can come and go with the single blast of a horn. Yet it still does damage.

Jet-skiing can be fun, but its loud buzzing sound can scare away wildlife as well as annoy people.

Noise pollution is a growing concern worldwide. Over the past one hundred years, noise pollution has steadily increased with the growth of cities. However, noise pollution can also affect any area that is in the flight path of a jumbo jet. High-pitched, loud and many different overlapping sounds all contribute to noise pollution. Indoors, household appliances hum, clocks tick, boards creak and water drips. Outdoors, it can be hard to escape the noise from traffic, construction equipment, pets and the general roar of everyday life.

Noise Over the Years

Noise is not a new complaint. More than 2,300 years ago in the ancient city of Sybaris, in what is now southern Italy, laws were passed to reduce noise. Over the last few centuries, as development and the use of machinery has increased, so has noise pollution. This trend is expected to continue as populations increase worldwide.

This photo shows a factory worker in 1923 using a drop-forging hammer, a noisy piece of machinery.

Efforts are being made to cut down on certain types of **noise pollution**. Airports have adjusted flight patterns to reduce the number of airplanes that fly over areas where many people live. Barriers have been built between motorways and people's houses to cut down on traffic **noise**. Local governments have passed laws limiting the use of leaf blowers, pneumatic drills and other gardening and construction equipment to certain times of the day. Vehicles have been modified to run more quietly.

The fuel-cell car is a recent development in the fight against noise pollution. The car is powered by hydrogen, not petrol, and it is noise- and pollution-free.

Noise: It's Against the Law!

Local governments around the world have passed laws designed to make their communities quieter. Here are just a few examples:

- Drivers can be fined in some places if the music from their car stereos is too loud.
- A neighbour heard fighting and screaming can be arrested, fined and jailed.
- The owner of a dog left outside to howl at the Moon all night can be fined or jailed.
- Many towns forbid owning cockerels. Even if a town allows cockerels, the law may limit the number that can be owned.

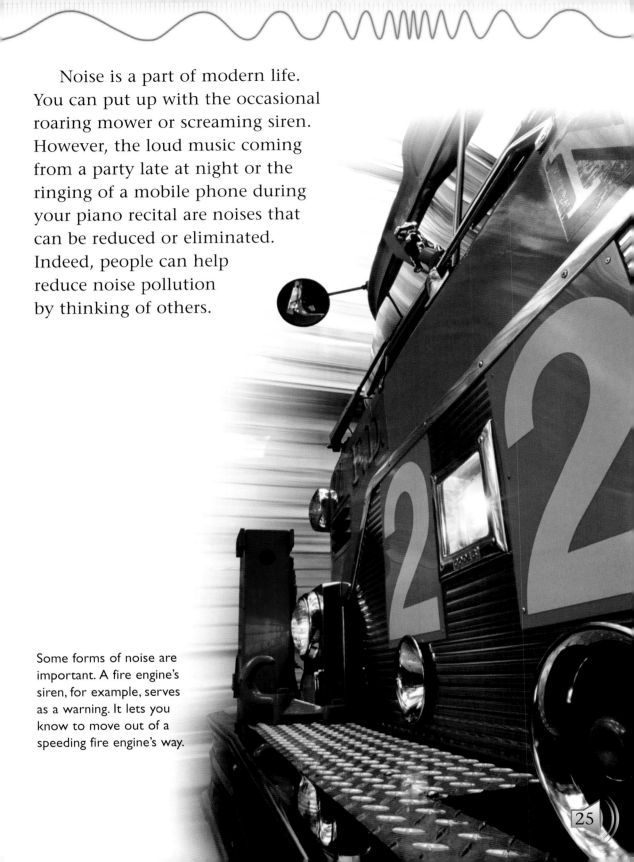

Noise is a part of modern life. You can put up with the occasional roaring mower or screaming siren. However, the loud music coming from a party late at night or the ringing of a mobile phone during your piano recital are noises that can be reduced or eliminated. Indeed, people can help reduce noise pollution by thinking of others.

Some forms of noise are important. A fire engine's siren, for example, serves as a warning. It lets you know to move out of a speeding fire engine's way.

Fighting Back Against Noise

Around the world, the message that **noise pollution** can be dangerous is being heard loud and clear. Many organizations are raising awareness about the problems of noise pollution and promoting hearing health. Here's just a small sample of what concerned people are doing to fight against **noise**.

Noise Action Day

Each June, people in the United Kingdom band together to fight noise on Noise Action Day. Organized by the National Society for Clean Air, a British environmental group, Noise Action Day is designed to encourage people to come up with simple solutions to noise problems. Many communities sponsor school programs about noise and hearing and civic programs about noise pollution control.

Teachers and pupils in Cardiff, Wales, turn out to support Noise Action Day.

Farm Noise and Hearing Project

The Farm Noise and Hearing Network recognizes that noise pollution is becoming more and more common in rural areas. The organization is made up of farmers and health care professionals from southern Australia. It sponsors the Farm Noise and Hearing Project, a campaign designed to educate residents of southern Australian rural communities about the dangers of noise.

Field days let farmers learn how to protect their hearing.

According to the organization, 60 to 80 per cent of farmers between the ages of thirty and seventy have suffered hearing loss caused by exposure to farm machinery. The project aims to reduce that number by making farmers aware of the dangers of loud farm noise. Members of the Farm Noise and Hearing Project sponsor field days and health events throughout southern Australia. They test farmers' hearing and give advice about ways that farmers can protect themselves from the dangers of noise.

This noisy combine harvester can make farmwork a danger to hearing health.

Hearing Education and Awareness for Rockers (HEAR)

Fifteen out of every thousand people under the age of eighteen have some form of hearing loss. Approximately 60 per cent of those inducted into the Rock and Roll Hall of Fame in Cleveland, Ohio, USA, have impaired hearing. HEAR is a non-profit group based in the United States. It was started by Kathy Peck, a rock musician who suffered hearing damage after performing in a concert in 1984. HEAR promotes information on hearing and hearing protection for musicians and music lovers. Members produce programs for school students and record television and radio announcements to raise awareness of the risks of amplified music.

From a distance of 1 to 2 metres, amplified rock music measures approximately 120 dB.

What You Can Do

Regulations that keep certain sources of **noise pollution** under control cannot completely restore peace and quiet to the world, nor can these regulations prevent all hearing loss. We must do our part to keep things quiet, too. What can you do about noise pollution?

- Be aware of the **noise** you make. For example, keep the volume low on your stereo, television and computer.
- Respect places in which calm and quiet are important, such as libraries, places of worship, restaurants and theatres.
- If you own a mobile phone, turn it off or set it to vibrate before entering quiet places. Remind your family and friends to do the same.
- Learn all you can about noise pollution and help educate your friends and family about its dangers.

Your mobile phone can be disruptive in places such as cinemas and libraries.

Other people's musical tastes may not be the same as yours – so keep it low.

Keep quiet in places such as libraries, where any noise can disturb others.

Are You Listening?

Noise pollution is not going to fade away. However, if you understand which sound levels can be dangerous and which sounds to avoid, you can minimize its harmful effects. You can protect your hearing and keep it healthy. Knowing how others might feel about the sounds that you are making will also make you a better neighbour.

If you do not take responsibility for protecting yourself and others from noise pollution, you may never hear the end of it!

These snowmobilers should be wearing ear protection.

Glossary

absorb   take in sound without reflecting it

amplify   make a sound stronger

compressed   squeezed together

crest   the highest point of a wave

decibel   a unit used to measure the relative loudness of sounds

noise   unwanted sound

noise pollution   annoying or harmful noise in an environment

reflection   sound that is turned or thrown back

sound waves   alternating low and high pressure vibrations that move through matter and are interpreted as sound in the ear

tinnitus   ringing or buzzing in the ears

trough   the lowest point of a wave

vibrates   moves backwards and forwards very quickly

Index